IMAGES OF ENGLAND

ROYTON

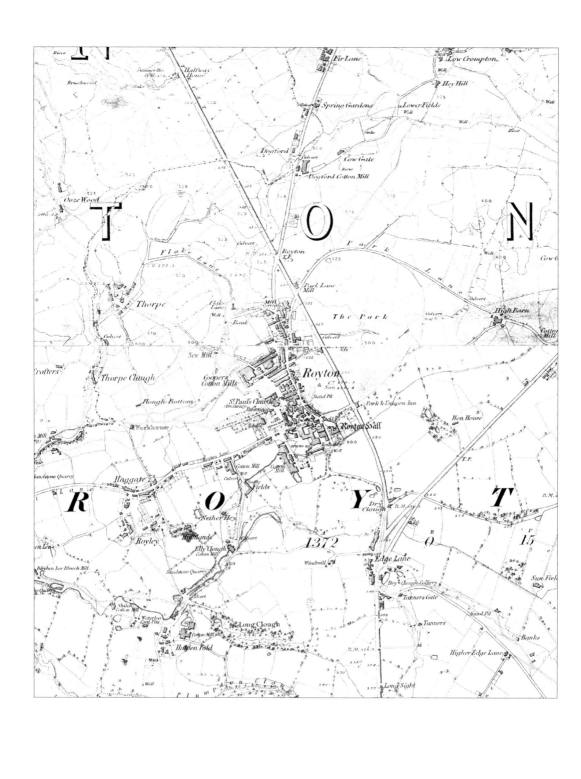

IMAGES OF ENGLAND

ROYTON

FRANCES STOTT

TEMPUS

Frontispiece: Royton from the Ordnance Survey map published in 1848.

First published 2005

Tempus Publishing Limited
The Mill, Brimscombe Port,
Stroud, Gloucestershire, GL5 2QG
www.tempus-publishing.com

British Library Cataloguing in Publication Data.
A catalogue record for this book is available from the British Library.

ISBN 0 7524 3516 7

Typesetting and origination by Tempus Publishing Limited.
Printed in Great Britain.

Contents

Acknowledgements

I should like to take this opportunity to thank the following people for the loan of their photographs: John and Kate (photographers), Rob Magee, Royton Library and the *Oldham Evening Chronicle* for access to their extensive collections, Father David Booth for the photographs of St Paul's church, the Revd D. Halford for photographs of St Anne's church, school and Edge Lane Hollow, Doug Ashmore, Bob Bishop, Brian Clegg, John Duff, Tony Edmondson, Gallery Oldham, Mike and Sheila Godfrey, Richard Grey (Seddon Atkinson), the late Olive Jones, Christine Kenyon, Emmeline Metcalf, Northern Mill Engine Society, Oldham Local Studies and Archives, Steve Rigby, the *Rochdale Observer*, Royton and Crompton School, No. 1855 Squadron Royton Air Training Corps (ATC), Tom and Freda Shaw, Margaret Slater, Ted Smith, Mike Smith (*Oldham Evening Chronicle*), Tony Spence, Jean Taylor.

Attempts have been made to trace the copyright owners of all photographs and the author wishes to apologise for any omissions which may have occurred.

In addition I should like to thank the following people for their information, advice, help and support: my husband Paul, Father David Booth, Marjorie Broadhurst, John and Cynthia Crothers, Heather Dunkerley, Nora Durham, Philip Hirst and the *Oldham Evening Chronicle*, Mike and Sheila Godfrey, Janet Green, Richard Grey (Seddon Atkinson), Gail Holden and the staff at Royton Library, Jean Howe, Arthur Kirby, David Lees (Crane Fruehauf), Rob Magee, Eric Meanock, Freda Millett, Keith Moores, Clive Newton, Freda Newton, Northern Mill Engine Society, the staff of Oldham Local Studies and Archives, Chris Orentas, John Orentas, John Phillp (Northern Mill Engine Society), Royton Cricket, Tennis and Bowling Club, Frank and Phyllis Schofield, Ted Smith, Tony Spence, Jean Taylor, Ted Westwood, David Winterbottom (Royton ATC).

In particular, I would like to thank Michael Higgins for sharing his knowledge of Royton's history.

Introduction

Royton was one of the many Lancashire towns to be caught up in the Industrial Revolution in the nineteenth century. Once dominated by a skyline of mills and their chimneys, most of which have now been demolished, it is hard to imagine that Royton has a history going back as far as 1212, when it was mentioned in a Survey of Lancashire, or even earlier if place names such as Thorp, which has Viking origins, are taken into consideration.

In the Middle Ages, Royton was a small village of scattered farming communities with Royton Hall, the home of the Byron family since the thirteenth century, at its centre. Records show that the Byrons were involved in all the major wars with Wales, France, Flanders, Scotland and Spain throughout the centuries, culminating with the English Civil War. By this time the Byrons had sold Royton Hall and made Newstead Abbey their home.

At the end of the Civil War, Royton was a rural community centred on the hall and surrounding farms. At this time there were forty-seven families in Royton, each eking out a living from farming the land and supplementing their income with the spinning and weaving of wool. The farms were small, pastoral in nature and dedicated to the rearing and grazing of cattle, with only a small amount of arable farming taking place, mostly producing potatoes, oats and turnips. A century later the village had begun to expand. The population of just over 1,000 lived in several hamlets which had become established in the village. Royton now boasted three woollen manufacturers and a fulling mill within its boundaries. The main hamlet in Royton was the district around the hall, St Paul's chapel and Sandy Lane.

Royton Hall in 1794, with St Paul's chapel and Tandle Hill in the background.

Royton Hall.

With its existing woollen heritage, Royton was ideally placed to take advantage of the introduction of a new fibre, cotton, and by 1776 woollen manufacture was in decline. King Cotton had arrived. Advances in textile manufacture (particularly the invention of Hargreaves' spinning jenny in 1764 and Crompton's mule in 1779) allowed Royton to expand from a domestic textile industry to one that was dominated by the mill. Royton was now firmly in the industrial age.

The first mills were built at Thorp Clough, followed in the 1780s by mills on the branches of the River Irk, which flowed through the township and Top of the Fold, opposite Royton Hall. By 1793 there were nine mills, five powered by water and four by horses. While carding and spinning were carried out in these mills, weaving remained very much a cottage industry. The development of the steam engine, coupled with plentiful supplies of coal (which had been found in the area of Royley, Oldham Edge and Streetbridge in the early eighteenth century) allowed further mill development. The first steam engine was installed in Edmund Wild's mill on Sandy Lane during 1806, and by 1832 there were twelve steam-powered mills in Royton. Three collieries also had steam engines, the one at Dryclough having three.

The cotton industry expanded as the demand for textiles rose, bringing about a transformation of all the Lancashire towns and villages. In 1785 Royton consisted of only a few mean-built and straggling houses, a workhouse (built in 1747), chapel (1754) and village school (1785). In 1793 there were 450 dwellings in the village, which had increased to 625 by 1811. By 1817 new regularly laid-out streets of brick-built houses were being constructed, which were soon to become commonplace. Gas lighting came to Royton with the building of the gas works on Union Street in 1832.

Royton's outlying hamlets were also expanding at this time. Streetbridge had a colliery and paper mill, Dogford a cotton mill, Dryclough had its windmill, malt kiln and coal mines, while Holden Fold was situated on a hill above a branch of the River Irk, which powered several mills and collieries in the valley below.

Transport services improved because of the need to import raw materials and for traders to access the Manchester markets. By the 1820s, for example, there was a regular 7.30 a.m. coach service from the Unicorn Inn on High Street to the Hare & Hounds at Shudehill in Manchester on Tuesdays, Thursdays and Saturdays. The inn was ideally situated, being on the then main road from Oldham to Rochdale. In the 1830s however, the new turnpike road between the two towns was extended, cutting through the former Royton Hall park and bypassing the centre of the village. From that time, the centre of the village began shifting to the east, straddling the new road. An 1840s proposal for a rail link by the Lancashire & Yorkshire Railway Co. came to fruition in 1864. Steam trams were introduced in 1883 and the line was electrified and upgraded in 1904. In 1895 the Oldham & Royton Canal Act was passed by Parliament, which proposed the construction of a canal leading off the Rochdale Canal at Castleton and terminating close to the centre of Royton. It was never built. Thirty years later road links were improved with the construction of Broadway, the new arterial road to Manchester, and more recently the construction of the M62 has provided access to the motorway network of the UK.

A Surveyor of Highways and an Overseer of the Poor originally governed Royton. The cotton famine brought poverty and hardship to Royton, and in 1863 the town invoked the 1858 Local Government Act and formed its own Local Board of twelve councillors. The Board was allowed to borrow money to provide employment for the out-of-work cotton operatives. Thornham was incorporated into the township in 1879 and three new councillors were appointed. The Local Board met in various locations before they built a fine town hall for themselves in 1880. In 1894 the Local Board became an Urban District Council, which was to administer the town for eighty years until the formation of Oldham Metropolitan Borough Council in 1974 brought the town's independence to an end.

The cotton trade passed through cycles of prosperity and recession. Despite the setbacks of the American Civil War, with the ensuing cotton famine resulting in the closure or the reduced working of many of the mills, together with the effects of the First World War, the cotton industry continued to expand until the 1920s when it went into terminal decline. Since that time, despite the industry making efforts to modernise, mills continued to close at a relentless pace and, with the closure of the Grape Mill in 2002, cotton spinning in the town ceased.

Royton Village School,
erected in 1785.

Royton, seen from Oldham Edge in September 1950.

The effects of the Second World War resulted in a temporary boom to the cotton industry. As in the First World War, women took on many occupations vacated by the men who had joined up. The town prepared for war by sandbagging the town hall, library and police station and building shelters as a precaution against air raids. One raid, on 30 August 1940, resulted in the bombing of the Belgium Mill, which was completely destroyed. Royton had its own Home Guard detachment, primarily recruited for the defence of the town, which guarded installations such as the railway station at night. Meanwhile the local population supported the various national fundraising campaigns for the war effort, including Dig for Victory, Scrap Metal Week, War Weapons Week and Warship week. The latter event raised £176,532 and resulted in Royton adopting HMS *Sparrow*.

During the post-war years many diverse industries established themselves in the town, including factories for the production of transformers, diesel vehicles, coachwork, automation equipment, rope and twine, wadding and kitchen and cafeteria equipment. Most of them in their turn have disappeared. Economic activity today is centred on small industrial estates and the Salmon Fields Employment Park, which includes major companies such as Slumberland and 3663, and the Centre Retail Park on the site of the former Elk Mill.

Royton has undergone many changes since the 1950s. Royton Council felt that the town, and particularly the houses and shops, were in need of renovation and so began a programme of major redevelopment, particularly in the central area. Terraced houses were pulled down and mills were either demolished or converted to other uses. Redevelopment saw many of the old independent churches disappear. The old main shopping street, Market Street, has been replaced by a new precinct containing twenty-three shops and a supermarket. The railway station with its warehousing and sidings has gone, replaced by housing. New estates (both council and private sector) have been constructed throughout the town, resulting in a population growth of 40% between 1961 and 1971. New schools have been constructed to provide education for the ever-growing population, which has continued to expand throughout the twentieth century and into the twenty-first century.

one

Royton Hall, St Paul's Church and School

Royton Hall was owned by the Byron family from the thirteenth century until around 1622, when they sold it to the Standish family, having by now made Newstead Abbey in Nottinghamshire their principal residence. Forty years later the Standish family sold the hall to the Percival brothers, Richard and Thomas. Thomas, a linen manufacturer, purchased his brother's share for £1,400 in 1670. His great grandson, also Thomas Percival, with his wife, Martha Gregge, refaced the hall in 1758. Their only child, Katherine, inherited the hall, which she left to her son William in 1765 when she died at the early

age of twenty-five. He in turn bequeathed the Royton Hall estate to his father Joseph Radcliffe in 1815.

Joseph Pickford was a noted magistrate who took strong measures to quell Jacobin riots in both Royton and Oldham in 1794 and 1795, and later against the Luddites in Yorkshire. He took the name Radcliffe in 1795 in order to inherit his maternal uncle's estate in Milnsbridge, near Huddersfield. The Radcliffe family later purchased Rudding Park near Harrogate, and this became the family's main residence.

After the Radcliffe family left Royton, they let the hall as tenements. From 1882 to 1900 part of the hall was used as the presbytery for SS Aidan & Oswald church, and from 1905 to 1910 St Paul's Institute was situated here.

FOR SALE BY PRIVATE TREATY

THE Ancestral Home of the Byron Family for over 400 years. Date of building unknown, but earliest historical reference of the Byron family at Royton Hall is 1262. The Hall is built of stone obtained from the foot of the Pennine Range, in the Saddleworth district, and the English oak used in its construction was obtained from the Chadderton Forest. There are two solid oak staircases, one being the oldest solid spiral oak staircase in Lancashire. For further description see following report dated 11/3/26, by W. H. Longworth, Esq., Architect, Manchester.

"The Mansion is an extensive one, the outer walls being constructed mainly of coursed stone with dressed stone ashlar forming the window heads, cills, and mullions.

The major portion of the Hall is Jacobean in character with the central portion Georgian in type.

Dressed stone flags have been utilised for the covering of the roofs and the weight of such material being very heavy has necessitated the utilisation of very stout oak timbers to give the necessary adequate support, and in these days when stone of this description is sought after for utilisation in modern house design the value of this material is considerable as the materials are in capital preservation, and it is very largely due to their hard-wearing qualities that one finds the oaken timbers comprising the roof timbers in so excellent a condition.

Further the external walls form a veritable quarry of worked stone, whilst the immense quantities of oak used in the construction of the roofs and floors must have much depleted the adjacent forest lands in that long past period when the Hall was in course of erection, and the stout manner in which the scheme was carried out once again confirms that our ancestors built for generations to come and not solely for their own days.

I have carefully examined the oak, and as previously stated it is astonishing to note the amount of this timber which has been used to form not only the roof timbers and floor joists but also the floorboards, and to find how very excellent its condition is after the lapse of centuries. Still it is English oak and consequently is famous for its lasting and wearing qualities.

The many ways in which such a huge quantity of English oak could be utilised comes to one's mind when going over the Hall, especially in these days when good quality English oak is so difficult to obtain except at a great cost.

One's hope that the whole of the panelling had not been removed is realised, there being a large quantity remaining of moulded oak panelling in capital condition of a type which is much sought after.

From a craftsmanship standard the excellently designed and carried out Georgian Staircase merits admiration with its moulded spandril, handrail, balusters, and newels, the whole of which is in splendid preservation.

The doors generally are in excellent preservation being formed of six panels and many of them are of oak.

A most unusual feature in the Hall is a spiral staircase leading from the Ground Floor to the Attics. It is especially interesting to note that the treads are formed out of solid oak, the tapered ends of which are framed into a circular oak column.

In what was probably the Retiring Room is a mantelpiece of Adams design with relief work and pilasters.

It is probable that in the event of demolition that some interesting finds may be made, as in many buildings of this type chambers formerly used as hiding places for fugitives are known.

In these days when good-class English oak is sought after, the vast amount of oak that has been utilised in the construction of Royton Hall together with the other items of value all tend to make the Premises a desirable acquisition to purchasers who deal in matters of this description.

It is on rare occasions that the opportunity is afforded of securing a Property the pulling down of which will release so much material which can be adapted to modern needs now that it has been decided to remove the structure."

The Hall can only be inspected by appointment. For any further particulars, etc. apply:—

Dr. J. T. GODFREY, ROYTON HALL, ROYTON, Near OLDHAM, LANCS.
Telephone No.: 311 Oldham.

Sales advert for Royton Hall, 1926.

Opposite, below: During the First World War, Royton Hall was used to house Belgian refugees. Two families arrived in October 1914: Mr and Mrs Byl and their five children from Ghent, and Mr and Mrs De Maeyer and their three children from Ostend. From left to right, back row: Mlle Marie De Maeyer, M. De Maeyer, Mme N. De Maeyer, M. Albert Byl, Mlle H. Byl, Mme Byl, M. Byl. Front row: Mlle Rosa De Maeyer, M.L. De Maeyer, Mlle R. Byl, Mlle J. Byl, and Mlle G. Byl.

Left: Dr John Thomas Godfrey, who died in 1935. A respected figure, Dr Godfrey was known locally as the 'Black Doctor'. He originated from Ceylon (Sri Lanka) and later moved to Durban, South Africa. He then moved to Scotland and trained at Edinburgh University. While studying there he met and married Elizabeth Marion Keene. The Godfrey's had four children, who were all educated at St Anne's in Royton. The hall was used both as his home and his surgery. Dr Godfrey first rented the hall from the Radcliffe family after the First World War, before finally purchasing the building in 1922. Dr Godfrey and his family returned to South Africa for two years in 1926 and upon their return moved to Southampton. Prior to his departure, he failed to sell the hall to either Manchester or Oldham Councils. Royton Council also refused the offer. Having failed to sell the hall, Dr Godfrey turned the building into tenements. By 1937 it was unoccupied and, on the advice of the Medical Officer of Health, the hall was placed under a slum clearance order and demolished in February 1939. Royton Council finally purchased the Royton Hall site in July 1961.

Opposite, below: St Paul's church in about 1882, with the Revd Richard Hill standing in the churchyard. In 1854 the church was lengthened by an additional bay at both the east and west ends, so incorporating the tower into the church. The organ and choir were moved to a new gallery at the east end of the chapel.

St Pauls Chapel, Royton. 1754

St Paul's chapel in 1754. Royton church was formerly a chapel of ease for the mother church at Prestwich. The site of the chapel and graveyard, Downey Field and Acre Field, were sold by Thomas Percival of Royton Hall on 9 August 1753 for the sum of one shilling. St Paul's was dedicated on 10 August 1754 and consecrated on 1 July 1757. The building was an oblong, grey-slated structure, built of brick and ornamented with stone cornices and quoins at the angles. In 1828 the chapel was enlarged with the addition of a square tower outside the original building at the west end, which was surmounted with a weather vane.

The Revd Richard Hill BA, vicar of St Paul's for thirty-eight years. The son of a farmer, he was born near Blackpool on 22 January 1816 and educated at Corpus Christi College, Cambridge. His first appointment was as curate at Bispham. He married Martha Higham of Whalley, near Blackburn, and in 1845 they moved to Royton. The Hills had five children, three daughters and two sons. During his ministry a day school was constructed, the church enlarged, the chancel added in 1883 and a mission church constructed at the top of Rochdale Lane. A school and mission room were also built at Edge Lane. Mrs Hill died on 1 February 1874 and Richard Hill died of apoplexy on 25 August 1883. He was interred in the vault in the church.

The interior of the old chapel, showing galleries, supported by slender iron columns, running on three sides of the building. Oak pews, some of which were square family pews, furnished the chapel. Just seen on the right is the 'Hall Pew', with its carved oak pillars and circular arches. The baptistery is on the right, at the rear of the church, with the 1754 font. Front left is the pulpit, an oak 'three-decker', the lower reading desk being used by the clerk and the upper portion by the clergyman. The brass eagle lectern was presented by the congregation in memory of the Revd R. Hill in October 1883.

Above: The church and graveyard in around 1885. The church was further enlarged in 1883 when part of the east wall was removed and a stone chancel erected (right). Miss Holden (of Launderbrook House, Shaw Street) defrayed the cost. In the burial ground could be found the grave of John Butterworth, 'Jack O' Ben's', who achieved national fame as a mathematician. He was born at Haggate, the tenth child of John and Anne Butterworth, on 16 February 1774. When John was six he was put to work on a Dutch wheel and he began weaving at the age of ten. He died on 3 December 1845. The highlight of his career was in 1826, when Thomas Telford entrusted him with the stress calculations of the new Menai suspension bridge.

Right: St Paul's church from Church Street in around 1920. The west window was dedicated on 15 April 1915 in memory of Joseph Higham Hill, son of the late Revd R. Hill, and his wife Hannah. Plans to almost totally rebuild the church in the Gothic style were made in 1887. The nave was demolished and a new enlarged one took its place. The two corner stones of the new church were laid on 6 April 1889, the first by Mrs John Holden of Highlands House and the second, with Masonic honours, by Colonel Le Gendre N. Starkie, RWPGM of East Lancashire and PGW of England.

Interior of the new parish church, *c.* 1900. The chancel arch is decorated in an ornate Byzantine style, while the doom, the area above the chancel arch, depicts Christ in Glory surrounded by angels. The east window was given by the Holden family in memory of John and Jane Holden and their sons George and John, of Launderbrook House in Shaw Street.

The modified interior, *c.* 1930. In 1919 the choir stalls were brought into the nave, the altar moved 6ft forward in order to create a choir vestry, and a marble floor and steps placed in the sanctuary. An oak rood screen incorporating the pulpit was erected between the front two pillars at the east end of the nave as a war memorial, which was dedicated on 1 September 1920.

As part of the church refurbishment in 1926, Adolphe Valette, well known for his paintings of Manchester, painted a new Christ in Glory on the doom. It was painted out around 1954. The church had a further facelift in 1970 when a new altar was installed in the centre of the church and the central section of the rood screen was moved to the rear of the church. The old altar was retained as a place for the reservation of the Blessed Sacrament.

Left: St Paul's church, seen from St Paul's Street.

Below: The old vicarage and Willow Cottage on Church Street with a procession, probably of those who had been newly confirmed, passing by. On 29 September 1761 Thomas Percival of Royton Hall granted to the chapel warden the New Brick House and a parcel of ground 'lying and being at the West End of the Chapel Yard at top of meadow commonly called or known by the name of the Cornfield' for the use of a 'Resident Minister at Royton, and for that purpose only', for the sum of one shilling a year. By the late 1890s, the building was dilapidated and it was decided to construct a new vicarage.

The new vicarage, church and graveyard at the turn of the century. Mrs Newton and Miss Holden of Highlands and church warden Robert Evans laid the foundation stones for the new vicarage on 13 September 1902. The vicarage was sold in the early 1990s and a new house purchased in Low Meadows. The churchyard was closed for burials in 1882, although internments into existing family graves continued until 1938. Royton Council took over responsibility for the graveyard in 1953 and undertook an improvement scheme in 1969. Nineteen of the 572 graves were retained and the whole area was landscaped.

Opposite, below: Royton church bazaar in Royton market hall. Church bazaars were a popular way of raising funds for various church building projects. The bazaar held in 1903 (to raise funds to pay for the new vicarage and proposed Church Institute) consisted of stalls representing England, Ireland, Scotland, Wales, Canada, Australia, India, Egypt, South Africa, Tasmania and the Army and Navy.

PARISH CHURCH INSTITUTE
ROYTON·

Ernest Woodhouse J.R.I.B.A.
Architect Manchester.

Above: The Church Institute had a number of homes before a purpose-built institute was constructed in 1910. The site chosen for the new building was that of 'Willow Cottage', adjacent to the vicarage. Building commenced in 1909 and the institute was opened on 30 July 1910. It included a reading room, billiard room (with space for two tables), games room and ladies room on the ground floor and an assembly room on the upper floor. In 1997 the building was sold and has since been converted into flats.

In 1785 public demand and subsequent public subscription led to the building of Royton Village School on a site to the east of St Paul's church. However, by the beginning of the nineteenth century the school proved to be too small, so it was decided to build a new and larger school at Chapel Croft, which was completed in 1833. The old village school continued to be used as a Sunday school. The two schools ran as one for four years until the clergy and trustees of Royton Village School had a disagreement, with the result that the trustees broke away and re-opened their own day school in the old building. The village school was enlarged in 1886 to celebrate its centenary. At the turn of the twentieth century the school became an infant school, and it finally closed on 26 September 1907, leaving only the Sunday school to continue. The last service at the Sunday school was on 12 January 1969, after which it closed and was subsequently demolished.

St Paul's Infant School, Downey House. In 1933 St Paul's School managers purchased Downey House, former home of the Cooper family, to be used as the infant school, the opening of which marked the centenary of St Paul's. A new junior school was built on Hindle Drive in 1977, and in 1998 the Hindle Drive School and Downey House School were amalgamated.

two

Civic Pride

Above: The town hall and market hall were built in 1880 and opened on 16 September by James Ashworth of Southport, the first chairman of Royton Local Board. The covered market was 112ft long and 58ft wide and was fitted out with stalls for about fifty tenants. It had a two-span roof with a row of pillars down the middle, and four shops formed the frontage. The entrance to the market hall was through the stone arch surmounted by a pediment. A glazed roof covered the space behind the archway. The clock and bell in the tower was the gift of Dr and Mrs J. Kershaw. The market hall was demolished in January/February 1957, with the exception of the retaining wall and the four shops on Rochdale Road.

Opposite, below: A 'traffic lorry', Royton Urban District Council's pride and joy, ordered on 2 December 1919 from J.B. Mills, who imported the 30/40cwt vehicle from the Traffic Motor Truck Corporation in St Louis, USA. The tipping wagon was fitted on its arrival. Royton Council bought the vehicle to replace one of their horses, 'Blossom', which was lame and considered unfit for further work.

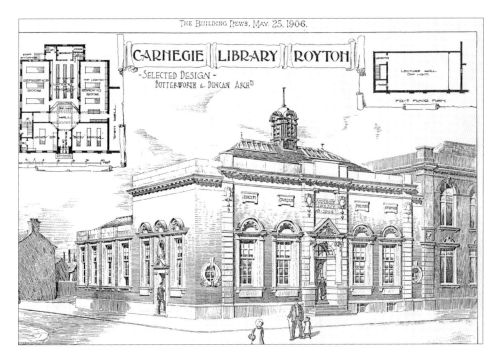

Above: The Carnegie Library. The library was opened on 12 January 1907 by Lord Stanley of Alderley. There had been numerous private libraries in Royton, which had been formed by groups of workers. These included the 'Circulating Library' (formerly the 'Jacobin Library'), formed in around 1794 and later based at the Hope and Anchor; 'The Select Library', established in 1823; and the 'Literary Institution', established in 1848. In 1902 the District Council applied to Andrew Carnegie for a grant, which was given in the October of that year. Carnegie was born in Scotland and moved to the USA in 1848, where he made his fortune. He firmly believed that wealth should be used for the good of the people, and established over 2,800 libraries. The Co-operative Society and the Liberal Club donated their collections of books to Royton's new public library.

Royton Baths, with the superintendent's house on the right. In 1908 the Council borrowed £7,500 in order to erect a public baths behind the library. Few doubted the need for a public baths in a town where most of the inhabitants were employed as textile operatives, and where few of the houses were fitted with a bath. However, it cannot claim to be the first public bath in Royton. Messrs Coopers, manufacturers, had erected a public bath for their workers in 1850 which was open to the public for 1d per bather. The bath was 30ft by 15ft and of various depths.

The swimming pool on the day of the opening. Cllr H. Beswick, chairman of the Baths Committee, opened the baths on 12 March 1910. The baths consisted of a swimming pool, slipper and shower baths for men and women, and a laundry. The opening ceremony was followed by a swimming gala, which included an exhibition of life-saving, a display of fast swimming by Henry Taylor and J.H. Tyers and an exhibition of high diving by H. Crank.

Royton Amateur Swimming Club in 1911. The club was founded in 1910, soon after the opening of the baths, and the following year the first students of the club's life-saving class passed their examinations and gained awards (twelve bronze medallions with certificates and five certificates of merit). The awards were presented by Cllr H. Beswick, president of the club, on 21 August to J.W. Howarth, H. Marland, J. Seville, S. Crothers, J. Penhall, F. Kent, W. Brassington, H. Dickinson, M. Chadwick, F. Bottomley, J. Schofield, J. Milne, H. Howarth, G. Howarth, H. Broadbent and I. Holland. In 1922 the club became a member of the Oldham and District Swimming and Water Polo League, and joined the Manchester and District Water Polo League in 1930, winning promotion to the first division in 1935.

The opening of Royton Park on Coronation Day, 22 June 1911. Cllr H. Roberts is presenting Cllr Z. Brierley, chairman of the Baths and Playground Committee, with a golden key with which to open the gates to the park. The park was on the site of the former Royton Colliery, which closed in 1901. The main entrance was on Whittaker Street.

The bandstand, which stood at the south-west end of the park. Regular brass band concerts were held during the summer evenings by bands such as Royton Public Subscription Band, Royton Public Brass Band and Shaw Prize Brass Band, as well as bands from further afield.

Looking down the main walk towards Rochdale Road. The drinking fountain, on the right, was situated at the junction of the main walk and the entrance from Radcliffe Street.

Opposite, below: On 10 May 1919, in the presence of a large number of people young and old, Royton was presented with a tank and a field gun from the First World War as a memorial to the war and the War Savings movement. The tank was presented by Lt-Col. P. Bamford of the 1/10th Battalion (Oldham) Manchester Regiment, on behalf of the War Office and the National War Savings Association. The 'lady' tank had been driven from the railway station by Lt Hepworth with Capt. Foster assisting. Miss Olive Jones can be seen in the foreground holding the post.

The drinking fountain bore the inscription 'Presented on the Coronation Day of George V by Mrs Tate and Miss Cooper in remembrance of the Cooper family of Downey House, Royton June 22 1911'. The fountain was made of red Melrose-Aberdeen granite and built by Mr J. Albert of Oxford Road, Manchester (the builders of White City, Manchester). In December 1960 it was decided to scrap the fountain, as the water pipes had perished and consequently the fountain had not worked for many years.

Tandle Hill Park and woods, consisting of 110 acres, were presented to the people of Royton by Norris Bradbury of Tynwald Mount, Royton on 6 September 1919 as 'A thank offering for peace after the Great European War 1914-19' (the date includes the Russian campaign against the Bolsheviks and the support of White Russians in 1919). Access to the park was via Oozewood Road, as it was not until 1924 that Tandle Hill Road was built as part of an unemployment scheme.

Walking in the park was a popular way of spending the day, particularly in summer.

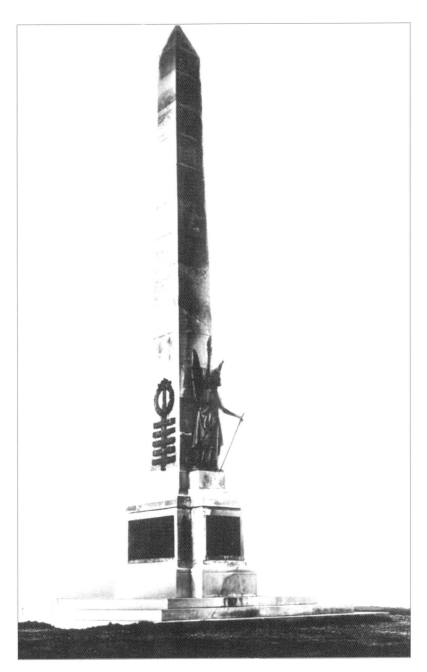

The war memorial was unveiled on 22 October 1921 by Lord Derby. It consists of an obelisk in Portland stone with a figure, the symbol of Peace, and ornamentations made of bronze designed by John Ashton Floyd. The names of those who died in the First World War were inscribed on three bronze tablets. The war memorial failed to withstand the Royton weather, however, and was taken down and replaced by one of granite in August 1924. The Second World War memorial plaques were unveiled on 25 July 1954. In 1967 vandals smashed the plaques and they had to be replaced. Two years later the plaques were stolen and replacement plaques were erected in St Paul's gardens in June 1970.

The entrance to the cemetery. The cemetery, covering an area of seven acres, was consecrated on 17 September 1879 by the Bishop of Manchester. There were three mortuary chapels, one each for the Church of England, Nonconformists and Roman Catholics. In 1924 the cemetery was extended by almost twelve acres.

Beating the Bounds, 14 April 1951. From left to right: Cllr G.L. Buckley, Walter Taylor, A. Donald Ogden (clerk to Royton Council), Julian Heywood, Jack Grindrod (rating officer), Cllr Charles Atherton, Cllr Charles Heywood, Mr T. Schofield, Frank Ashworth, J. Douglas Ramsden. In the days before detailed maps were available, the town's boundaries were beaten every ten years to remind people where the boundaries lay. The Beating of the Bounds in Royton was resurrected in October 1908 after a lapse of fifty years. The ten-year custom was again overlooked, as the next event did not take place until 1 October 1923. After a further lapse it was revived on 14 April 1951, 23 September 1967 and finally on 31 March 1974.

three

Royton Centre

Rochdale Road with the gabled police station on the left and the town hall, market centre and Royton Industrial Co-operative Society's drapery and outfitters on the right.

Opposite, above: No. 65, a standard four-wheel open-topped electric tram car on Oldham Road. Steam trams from Royton to Oldham commenced in August 1885 and ran on a 4ft 8½in gauge. This caused problems, as the existing line from Rochdale to Royton was 3ft 6in gauge, meaning that there could be no through trams from Rochdale to Oldham. The two sets of tracks met at Dogford Road and the depot there had to accommodate vehicles of both gauges. The trams from Rochdale used the entrance on Dogford Road while the larger entrance in Schofield Street was for the Oldham trams.

The last steam tram ran from Boundary Park through Royton on 5 November 1903, and the following day conversion to electricity began. The work was completed on 1 November 1904, and a through service commenced from Hathershaw to Summit, where it met the trams from Rochdale. Route numbers were introduced in March 1921, replacing the old coloured light system. The Hathershaw to Summit line was route No. 7. Trams were replaced by motor buses on this route in 1926, only to be re-introduced on 1 May 1928. The trams were finally replaced on 6 November 1937.

Below: Prior to the introduction of rural police constables on 24 July 1840, Royton had two constables chosen from the inhabitants, and appointed annually by the Vestry meeting. In December 1854 tenders were requested for the construction of this police station and court house, which was constructed on Rochdale Road. It was rebuilt in 1904/05 on the same site, and again in 1984 on Radcliffe Street.

Royton Conservative Club, Byron Street, at the turn of the century. The club was formed in the early 1860s. Its first home was in a wooden building at Bull Ring, Royley. Their stay there was short-lived, as the land was required for agricultural purposes. Their next home was erected in a field near Mill Lane, Haggate. It was decided, however, that a location near the centre of Royton should be sought, and in 1867 the club moved to the upstairs rooms in the Literary Institute on Sandy Lane. The following year they moved to Cooper's old baths below Downey House, and in 1893 it was decided that more up-to-date premises were required, and the present site on Byron Street was acquired. The club moved into their new headquarters in January 1896. In 1971 the building was destroyed by fire and a new club was built on the site two years later.

Looking up High Barn Street. On the left is the Union Bank of Manchester, now Barclays Bank. The Royton Spinning Co.'s mill is in the centre of the photograph, and Royton station to the right. The Lancashire & Yorkshire Railway branch line to Royton was completed in 1863. After 103 years the station closed on 16 April 1966. As well as the passenger station there was a large goods yard and warehouse, used to store the raw cotton brought by train from Liverpool docks prior to delivery to the local mills.

High Barn Street with High Barn Farm on the left at the top of the unmade road. The farm later became the clubhouse for Crompton and Royton Golf Club. The road was extended from the golf club to Luzley Brook as part of an unemployment scheme in 1924.

Above: Station horses on parade. The railway station was always a hive of industry. Around 1910 there were approximately 300 coal wagons in the bays at the station, and the local coal merchant's offices backed onto High Barn Street. The horse-drawn coal wagons, box carts and lorries went in and out of the station yard throughout the day, supplying both mills and households.

On Wednesday 8 February 1961 the occupants of three houses were rudely awakened at 6.15 a.m. when the early morning train crashed through the buffers at Royton Station, crossed High Barn Street and buried itself in their homes. The driver jumped from his cab as the train went through the station and suffered severe head injuries, including a fractured skull. None of the five people in the houses were seriously injured.

Opposite, below: Oldham Road. The Railway Hotel (originally called The Unicorn and Park Inn) was built by William and Susannah Ogden, who had run the Unicorn Inn on High Street. To the right of the public house is Duckworth's grocer's shop. The shops and terraced houses were demolished in 1973 to make way for the final part of the Royton Hall estate development.

J.H. Wilson advert from 1917.

Central Garage,
ROYTON nr. OLDHAM

Telephone 237.

Wilson's Motors (Royton) Ltd.

**AUTOMOBILE ENGINEERS,
AGENTS and REPAIRERS.**

Charabanc Tours
15, 18, 28 and 33 Seaters.
Now Booking for 1921 Season.

Motor Haulage
and Household Removals

**Taxis and Private Cars for Hire.
Ford Agents and Ford Service Depot.**

**Agents for
DUPLEX
Cars**

Dennis and A.E.C. Commercial Vehicles.

J.H. Wilson (now Wilson's Motors) advert from 1920.

Frank Schofield's Acme Press on Oldham Road in 1930. Mr Schofield used the stable on the right as his printing works. The building is currently occupied by Oldham Hire Centre.

The Carters' Arms in 1921. Harry Allen was the landlord here for only a few months. The public house probably took its name from the occupation of the first landlord, William Holdroyd, who in addition to running the public house was also a hay dealer and carter. Virtually all the men are sporting a flower in their buttonhole.

The top of Middleton Road, May 1965. The Percival coat of arms can just be made out on the corner of Shepherd Street.

Middleton Road, looking up towards the crossroads. On the right between the shops is the rear entrance to Royton Hall. Middleton Road was originally called Pickford Street (from the crossroads to High Street), Fleet Street (from High Street to Chapel Croft), Haggate Lane (from Chapel Croft to Holden Fold Lane) and Royton Lane (from Holden Fold Lane to Mill Lane).

Above: Co-op pork butcher's cart on Hall Street, decorated for the Oldham carnival in around 1928.

Right: Royton Congregational church after the renovation of the organ and re-decoration of the church in 1948. A celebrity concert was held and the church organ was first played by BBC organist Sandy Macpherson. This was the second time that the organ, introduced in 1875 to replace a harmonium, was rebuilt.

The old cottage on Fleet Street, where local poet James Taylor (1794-1863) was born. James was the eldest son of John Taylor, formerly of Luzley Brook. As a child he had no formal schooling and used to help his mother 'bat' cotton, which she picked in preparation for spinning. At ten he was operating a handloom. In 1818, when he was twenty-four, he met his cousin William Fitton, a surgeon and noted reformer, who advised him to learn to read and write. He sought the help of Margaret Bottomley (known as Peggy Street), who kept a small village school, and through her he learned to read and write. Within seven years he had produced a book of miscellaneous verse, which was published by Blackwoods. He is most noted for his poem *On My Native Village*.

Mrs Mellor's house on Fleet Street (later 51 Middleton Road). It was here in May 1857 that a meeting was held to discuss the establishment of a Co-operative Society in Royton. The society's first shop was in Sandy Lane, and in 1861 they purchased that building along with two adjacent properties. In 1907 Mrs Mellor's house had become a shop selling drapery, sheets and shirts.

The Independent Order of Oddfellows' club on Union Street, around 1930. On 22 March 1830, a lodge (known as the Loyal Farmers Lodge No. 419) was formed at the Hope and Anchor public house. They later moved to the Cemetery Inn (now the Travellers Rest), before moving to these premises on Union Street in July 1894. Meanwhile, the Carders Refuge Lodge 2020 was formed on 23 November 1839 at the Greyhound Inn (it later moved to the Spread Eagle). The two Lodges amalgamated to form the Loyal Farmers and Carders Lodge on 1 January 1923.

Charles Street, *c.* 1910. This was the 'chic' part of Royton, where mill managers, engineers, trade salesmen and buyers lived.

High Street in the early 1960s. The building at the bottom of the picture, the gents' toilet, was known locally as the 'round house'. On the gable wall are adverts for many well-known products.

High Street, September 1961. On the left are old hand-loom weavers' cottages. The houses were demolished in the early 1970s.

St Paul's Street, with St Paul's church in the background, *c.* 1910. On the left is the Blue Bell, which closed in 1970. The houses on the right were demolished in 1935 to make way for Jubilee Gardens.

St Paul's Street from Jubilee Gardens. The Blue Bell public house is on the left.

Unicorn Inn in festive mood around 1910, advocating that people should support Royton charities. The inn closed in 1912 and the building became a lodging (doss) house. It was demolished in the 1940s.

The top of St Paul's Street (where it met Thorp Road) on 27 May 1935. To the left (out of sight) is St Paul's church and graveyard. The two houses in the centre were built in 1846. The house on the left used to be occupied by Thomas Woolfenden, teacher at the Village School and later Registrar of Births and Deaths.

Right: William Taylor's cotton factory (or 'engine house') on 27 May 1935, just prior to demolition. The factory was built around 1793. Taylor owned all of the property on Cotton Street, which presumably took its name from the occupation of his tenants, who cleaned raw cotton by hand prior to spinning on a hand mule. They also undertook all of the reeling for Taylor's other mill on Dogford Road.

Below: Cotton Street on 27 May 1935. William Taylor also built the Bethesda Particular Baptist church (left) on Cotton Street in 1775. Worship continued here until a new church was built at the bottom of Dogford Road in 1860. Royton's fire brigade was to have its headquarters here in later years. In Cotton Street you could also find a day school, ambulance classes and a dancing school.

Croft Head. In the centre is Cocker's grocer's shop, with Thomas Turner's fruit shop on its right. The price of several groceries can be seen in the window. Butter was 10d per pound, and rich tea was 1s 6d.

Jubilee Gardens, looking towards Sandy Lane. The gardens stand on the site of property which had been the subject of a slum clearance order. William Cheetham, of Fern Bank on Dogford Road, presented the gardens to the town in 1937 in commemoration of the Silver Jubilee of the late King George V in 1935.

Above: Sandy Lane in 1970, just prior to its demolition. The building on the left is Varley's the printers, who published the *Royton Annual* from 1901 to 1942. Four doors up from Varley's was Clifford Clee's newspaper shop. The newsagents was thought to be 100 years old, and believed to be the oldest newspaper shop in Royton.

Right: The interior of Varley's printers shop in 1901.

Above: The Hope and Anchor in November 1958. The row of houses adjacent to the public house was demolished soon after this photograph was taken. The Hope and Anchor was already in existence in 1794, when records show that the 'Jacobin Library' at the Light Horseman was transferred here. The collection had been formed by workers, shopkeepers and small manufacturers, and after its transfer to the Hope and Anchor it was renamed 'The Circulating Library'. In 1850 it comprised 650 volumes, with the eighteen members each paying 6d a month towards its upkeep.

Left: Hancock's cobblers shop at 64 Sandy Lane.

Opposite, below: The Hare and Hounds on Sandy Lane was built in about 1790 by John Coates, who used the top floor for fustian cutting. Sometime before 1805 he converted it into a public house, which closed in 1917. In the 1920s Royton's Band and Social Club moved here from Chapel Street. Demolished in the 1960s, the club moved to new premises across the road in March 1964.

Above: Nos 61 to 65 Sandy Lane. The numerous mullioned windows of the top storey, most of which are bricked up now, indicate that these were loom houses. The windows allowed the maximum amount of light into the work area, to enable the weavers to work at their looms. The houses, the last of their kind in Royton, were about 200 years old when they were demolished in 1966.

Whittaker's Yard, Sandy Lane in November 1958. The area was named after the Whittaker family, who were cotton mill entrepreneurs and owners living at Fleak House (later Lower House) and Higher House (also the home of the Mellor family). Henry Whittaker owned the mill on Hall Street. A descendent, Robert Whittaker, lived at Brooklands on Rochdale Road, just to the north of Higher House.

Two charabancs, complete with day-trippers, outside the Junction Inn. This was probably the outing of forty-six people to Chester on 27 July 1924, paid for by landlord Robert Howarth. Two companies in Royton had charabancs for hire: Royton Motor Co. on Dogford Road, and Wilson's Motors at Central Garage. The vehicle on the left is a Dennis.

Old Peggy Street's dame school on Thorp Road. Peggy's real name was Margaret Bottomley, and it was she who taught the poet James Taylor to read and write in 1818. Margaret, aged sixty, was listed as a schoolmistress in the 1841 Census. In the Poor Rate of the 1830s and 1840s, the weaver James Bottomley was renting the cellar of a house in Thorp Road.

Above, left: The brick-built Wesleyan chapel on Chapel Street was founded in 1804, and opened on 1 September the following year. Thomas Cooper, a grocer and corn dealer on Sandy Lane whose descendants built Downey Mill and Downey House, paid for the construction. The old chapel was demolished around 1925. When a new Wesleyan church (below) was built on Market Street in 1874/5, the old chapel became the Philharmonic Institute. The institute was occupied by several organisations, including Royton's Band and Social Club and the Salvation Army. Royton's first Salvation Army commanding officer was appointed in 1886, and in 1919 they were recorded as being situated on Park Street. The Salvation Army later moved to Spring Garden Street and erected their own hall. The foundation stone for a new hall, adjacent to this, was laid on 14 September 1935 and the hall was opened on 13 June the following year by Mrs J.W. Smethurst. In 2004 the Royton branch amalgamated with the Shaw branch and the citadel on Spring Garden Street was closed in December of that year.

Left: St John's Methodist church and school, *c.* 1910. The last service in the church, built in 1874/5, was held on 21 January 1968 and four months later the church was demolished to make way for the town centre redevelopment project. Until their new church on Radcliffe Street was built, the congregation attended the Methodist church on Oldham Road. The new church, Trinity, opened in May 1971, replacing not only St John's but also Haggate and Oldham Road Methodist churches.

Children of Royton Wesleyan (St John's) Day School, *c.* 1890.

Laying the foundation stones for the Wesleyan Sunday school extension on 9 July 1910. Sixteen corner stones were laid by members of the church. Five hundred and eighty teachers, scholars and members of the church formed a procession in Market Street, headed by the Wesleyan Boy's Life Brigade, Shaw Wesleyan Boy's Life Brigade and Edge Lane Wesleyan Boy Scouts. The extension (consisting of a Young Men's Institute, ladies parlour, secretary's room, kitchen, five classrooms, a crush hall and toilets) was opened on 10 December 1910 by Thomas Burton.

Above: Market Street, *c.* 1905. John Bent's tripe dealer's shop is on the left.

Left: The Albion Club on King Street in 1972. Although the club opened in 1872 as a cotton exchange for mill owners and mill managers, membership of the club was later extended to include members from all walks of life. The club was demolished to make way for the town centre redevelopment, and a new club was opened on 10 October 1973 by its president, John Warby.

four

Surrounding
Districts

Thorp at the turn of the century. The building on the right, partially painted white, is Thorp Farm, which was demolished in 1976.

When Thorp Farm was demolished, a cruck frame was discovered on the right-hand gable end. Crucks were usually set 15ft apart like pillars in a church. Cross-bars were then placed from one upright to the other, forming roof trees and rafters. Between the uprights, hurdle work of wattle (daubed with clay and straw) formed the walls, which were then painted white on the outside. When the wattle perished, the walls were re-formed with stone. To convert this type of building into a two-storey structure was difficult, as the roof trees could not be removed. In Thorp Farm, the roof trees were 36in above the chamber floor, meaning that the owners had to bend double when going to bed.

The old Manor House in ruins, *c.* 1943. The headstone on the house bore the following inscription:

T

R A

AD 1671

The 'R' and the 'T' stand for Ralph Taylor.

This early seventeenth-century building was known as 'The Chapel'. It was situated almost at the corner of the crossroads formed by the roads leading to Tandle Hill, Thorp Clough, Dogford and Croft Head. The date stone would have been put in place when the building was converted from wattle to stone. It stood in its own grounds at the back of Taylor's manor house, and was known for its fine steel-studded oak door, which was stolen in 1914. Before the building was demolished it was used as a loom house.

The old house and workshop which lie at the bottom of the common known as Pingling Pit are relics of the felt hat trade in Royton. The common would have been used by the crofters to graze their animals and by their children to play games. The cottage on the left, with smoke coming out of the chimney, used to be the Gardener's Arms public house.

The former Royton workhouse, situated at the bottom of Mill Lane and now converted into cottages.

Stove, Royley Clough. On 11 July 1927 water poured down from Summit and Oldham Edge, leaving most of the low-lying areas of Royton under water. The Holly Mill lodge also burst its banks, adding to the floodwaters heading to Streetbridge. Cottages lying on the banks of the River Irk suffered serious flood damage.

The River Irk flowing through Royley Clough. Millfield Cottage, home of the owner of Royton Mill, can be seen in the background.

The original Royley House with Mr Smith, the gardener. Royley House bore the date 1652 and the initials of J. & A. Rhodes, to whom the Royley estate once belonged in the days of the Commonwealth. To the left of this photograph was the Victorian extension, built onto the old house by the Holden family in 1877. The old part of the house later became known as Royley cottages, and the property was demolished in 1958.

Royley Farm, cottages and part of the shippon (cattle shed). Above the door of the shippon can be seen a date stone bearing the inscription '1732' and the initials 'J.J.H.' with two stars, the rose and the thistle.

Looking up Middleton Road from what is known locally as 'Scotch'. Haggate House is at the top of the hill on the right.

Haggate Farm in 1913. The farm stood opposite the present Haggate public house on Middleton Road.

Above: The Greyhound Inn in Elly Clough, seen here in the 1930s, when John Smith was the landlord (1932-38).

Right: A mission (connected with St Anne's) was started in a rented cottage at Holden Fold in 1907. The cottage was considered unsuitable, and this small iron church, which cost £250 to build, was opened on 25 April 1908. Dedicated to St Cuthbert, it was known locally as the 'tin mission'. It closed in 1927.

St Anne's church. The stone-laying ceremony, by Miss C.M. Cocker of New Bank, Shaw, took place on 27 June 1908. Edge Lane Hollow, Thomas Street and the surrounding area were festooned with banners and bunting. The church, designed by Mr W. Temple Moore of London in fourteenth-century English Gothic style, was consecrated on 27 January 1910 by the Bishop of Manchester, Dr E.A. Knox. The upper portion of the tower was not constructed until 1927.

Members of the congregation on 26 January 1910, ready to prepare St Anne's church for its consecration the following day. When the church was first opened there was no money to pay for a caretaker or cleaner, so every Friday night the young women of the church used to dust and clean it.

Royton and the rear of Edge Lane Hollow from Robert Street, which was renamed St Anne's Avenue in about 1912. On the skyline to the left is SS Aidan & Oswald presbytery and church.

Edge Lane Hollow. The three-storey former mill building is occupied by Robinson sign writers. Edge Lane Hollow formed part of the original road from Oldham to Rochdale prior to the construction of the turnpike road in the 1830s. The old road ran over Oldham Edge and along Old Edge Lane, the Hollow, Plain Nook (now Roman Road), Hall Street, High Street, Sandy Lane, Rochdale Lane, Dogford Road, Fir Lane, Narrowgate Brow and Castleton Road before continuing to Rochdale.

Looking towards Oldham. The three-storey building in the centre of the photograph is a lodging house. The first vicar of St Anne's, the Revd J.T. Ormerod, used to visit the men who lived there. One Sunday afternoon he brought the men into the church, locked the door and baptised them all.

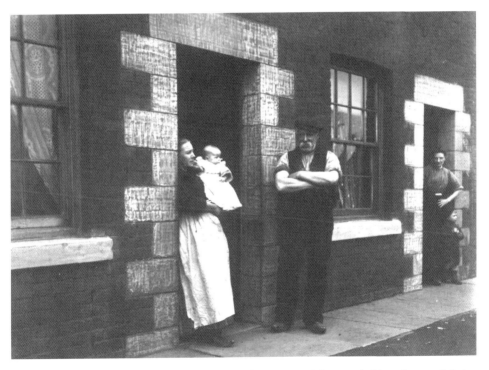

The cottages and lodging house in Edge Lane Hollow were mainly occupied by miners and their families. The men worked at the nearby Edge Lane and Dryclough collieries, while their families were employed in the cotton mills.

The lowest part of Edge Lane Hollow. In 1910, managers at St Anne's School on Old Edge Lane were notified that better accommodation was required for the school. As a result it was decided to construct a new building, rather than improve the old one. The best site was that between the church and the main road, and the Revd Ormerod was eventually able to purchase the Hollow for £2,000. Proposals had already been put forward in 1911 to improve Edge Lane Hollow by demolishing the old property, closing the old road and filling it up to the level of the new road.

Royton's windmill was unique, as there are no records of any other windmill in the area (the local corn mills were generally water-powered). According to the title deeds, the land on which the building stood was taken on lease in July 1794 for the erection of a windmill or other building. A malt kiln was later erected alongside it. On 4 August 1795 a mob marched from Saddleworth through Oldham to Edge Lane corn mill in Royton with the intention of destroying it. However, they were prevailed upon by the windmill owner to abandon their intention and they returned to Oldham to terrorise the shopkeepers there and compel them to lower the price of their provisions. It was demolished it in 1951.

Above: The foundation stone of the new St Anne's School was laid on 31 October 1914 by Miss Catherine Ormerod, and the school was opened on 2 November 1916. In January 1929, St Anne's became a 'central school' for senior children, and it became necessary in 1933 to build a new infant school on the north side of the church. It opened the following year. In 1944 St Anne's became a secondary modern school, which was amalgamated with High Barn and Newbarn Central Schools in 1967 to form Royton and Crompton Comprehensive School at Luzley Brook. The former secondary school was then modernised, a cloister-type quadrangle was built and the building was once again re-opened as a primary school.

Left: When the new school was planned it was also decided to erect a wayside cross, and with the outbreak of the First World War it was decided to make the wayside cross into a war memorial to the men of St Anne's. Standing at the entrance of what was to become Broadway, the cross was unveiled by Mrs Ormerod on 12 November 1921. Unfortunately a lorry demolished the cross in January 1938, and the base now lies in St Anne's churchyard.

EDGE LANE BREWERY AND BOTTLING CO.,

Edge Lane Brewery, ROYTON.

BREWERS AND BOTTLERS.
WINE AND SPIRIT MERCHANTS.

Bitter and Strong Ales always in Stock.
Bottlers of Bass's Pale Ale and Barley Wine.
Burton Ales and Guinness's Stout (Harp Label).
Bass's Draught Beer always in Stock.

All orders receive prompt attention at reasonable prices.
Goods always in condition.

Left: An sdvert for Edge Lane Brewery, 1926.

Below: An Edge Lane Brewery dray wagon. Built by Haworth Ratcliffe in 1884, Edge Lane Brewery was situated on Jones Street. In the 1890s it was registered to Fletcher Travis & Co. Ltd. Taken over by Oldham Brewery in 1895, the business was repurchased by Fletcher and Travis two years later. The company was wound up in 1916 and the brewery was bought by H. & A. Beswick, who renamed the business the Edge Lane Brewery & Bottling Co. The brewery finally closed in about 1939.

William Fitton, a barber, on Old Edge Lane in 1938. The building on the right is Edge Lane Foundry, previously Edge Lane Mission, which adopted the name St Anne's in 1896.

Shaw Road End. The shop on the corner of Shaw Road and Oldham Road is Newton's pharmacy, which also had a branch at Croft Head.

Dryclough Manor was built by the Evans family, proprietors of the Edge Lane Colliery. The colliery was owned by Evans, Barker & Co. in the 1850s, and later by the Oldham, Middleton & Rochdale Coal Co. In 1901 Dryclough Manor was the only property owned by them, the coal mine having closed some time earlier. In the late 1980s Dryclough Manor was converted into a residential home.

Mellor & Matthew's tobacconists at 164 Shaw Road, *c.* 1915.

Shaw Road, Luzley Brook, looking towards Shaw.

Luzley Brook at the junction of High Barn and Blackshaw Lane in 1938.

The Flowerpot Inn on Higginshaw Lane in the 1890s, when James H. Sutcliffe was the landlord.

William IV Row. Left of centre is the three-storey William the Fourth public house which was built before the turnpike road. As a result, you had to go down several steps to the level of the original road before entering it. The nine cottages on the right were built at a later date.

The Rose of England at Moss Gardens, Higginshaw, sometime between 1903 and 1906. The public house was 400 years old, originally thatched, and probably started its life as a farmhouse. There used to be a small lake at the front and a bowling green to the rear. It was demolished at some point between 1910 and 1922.

The Lancashire Hotel, Higginshaw Lane, in 1951. The public house was once a cottage beerhouse, situated behind the present public house. It was probably built of mud and bricks, like the Rose of England originally was. The building is now occupied by Healing International Travel.

An aerial view of Higginshaw in June 1976. In the background
is the Higginshaw gasworks, in front of which is the Crane
Fruehauf works, with their trailer park to the left. Middle left
is the Woodstock factory. The long building in the centre of
the photograph is Seddon Atkinson's flow line, with the Rhos
works in the rear. In the foreground are the Pennine works.

Old Buff Farm in the 1920s. The farm was built in 1702, and was the home of Ralph Taylor, the brother of Edmund Taylor of Thorp. In the 1920s and '30s the stable on the left was used as a joiner's shop by E. Davies. The billboard is advertising two silent films at the King's Cinema; *Fear Market* (starring Alice Brady) and *Riddle Woman* (starring Geraldine Farrar and Montagu Love).

The Friends meeting house (built in 1884) and burial ground at the top of Turf Lane. This meeting house, which was paid for by Thomas Emmott JP of Oldham and his sisters Elizabeth Emmott and Mary Ann Barlow, replaced the former meeting house, which had fallen into disrepair. Although the meeting house was demolished in 1939, the cemetery still remains as a small garden.

Above: Dr Kershaw's cottage hospital was provided and endowed in 1931 under a bequest by Dr John Kershaw, who died in 1909. It was opened on 28 February 1931 and transferred to the Oldham and District Hospital Management Committee in 1948 under the National Health Act. In the 1970s it became famous as a result of the work of Patrick Steptoe and Robert Edwards: the conception of Louise Brown, the first test-tube baby. In 1988 Dr Kershaw's hospital was designated as a hospice.

Right: John and Eliza Smith with their son Edmund outside their butcher's shop, which was situated on the corner of Oldham Road (originally Quaker Lane) and Clarence Street, *c.* 1890

Left: Deborah Travis (later Mrs William Knyvett) was born at Shawside on 31 December 1796, and in her later years lived at Hey Cottage, Heyside. She died on 10 January 1876. In her youth she trained for five years with the Ancient Concerts Society in London, and made her debut singing before the Prince Regent. She was renowned for her singing of Handel oratorios, and performed throughout the country. Elizabeth Gaskell mentioned Deborah in her novel *Mary Barton*, published in 1848.

Below: Congregational Sunday school on Hebron Street in 1901.

St Mark's church prior to the construction of the vicarage in 1909. Built in the Early English style, the foundation stone was laid on 30 March 1877 by Mrs Macdona and consecrated on 15 May 1878. An iron mission room, St Chad's, was erected at Higginshaw in 1894.

Old Chittie Farm, a three-storied loom house on Oldham Road. It was so-called because of the apprentice 'chitties', orphans from the Duke of York School in London, employed there by Jonathan Buckley. He mistreated the children so badly that in 1820 he was arrested, tried and sentenced to two years' imprisonment. The farm was later occupied by the Wellock family, who are shown in this photograph. The farm was demolished in 1953/4.

Robert Wyld's barn, at the top of Water Street. In 1672 the barn was licensed as a Nonconformist meeting place, but the license was withdrawn the following year and the barn was converted into a house. The Manor House, built around 1580, is the building on the right. Its only door was at the side, as it had a garden that ran up to the main road. It was occupied by Benjamin Travis, the second vicar of Royton and uncle of George Travis, who was born in the house next door and later became Archdeacon of Chester.

Old cottages in Water Street. They were demolished in the early 1950s and replaced by bungalows.

Lower Fold Farm dates back to 1530. Originally known as Cheetham's Cross, Lower Fold Farm's date stone was inscribed 'RC 1638 TC'. When a portion of the old Lower Fold Farm fell down in 1925, it exposed an outer stone wall with an inner wall 18in thick, built with small stones and mud.

This photograph is taken from Three-Acre Field. The land in the foreground was a meadow, while the trees were planted over the top of drift mines to prevent the farmer taking heavy carts over them. The farmhouse and buildings were demolished in 1953/4.

Intake Farm, on Bull Cote Lane, was built in 1742, and was supposed to have been erected by the Cockers to serve as a vicarage to Shaw chapel. The porch at the front was used as a cheese-pressing room. In 1911 the farm consisted of a house, farm buildings and thirteen acres of meadow and pasture.

The mission church of All Saints, which was attached to St Paul's, was opened on 28 February 1875, the foundation stone having been laid the previous year by the Revd R. Hill. Services were discontinued in 1890 for a period of six years. New classrooms were built in 1907.

The interior of All Saints church. The pulpit on the left is from the old St Paul's church.

The corner of Dogford Road and Rochdale Road, with T.H. Shepherd's baker's shop on the corner. Shepherd's began with Mr Shepherd going door to door selling bread made by his wife. He eventually bought the shop and had his bakery round the corner on Schofield Street. By 1900 he had five horse-drawn vans delivering bread daily. Ibbetson Lumb took over the Schofield Street bakery around 1917, although the shop continued under Shepherd's ownership. Mr Shepherd died in May 1922. For many years he had been the choirmaster at the Wesleyan church, and he was a soloist of some repute.

Ibbetson Lumb's delivery van on Schofield Street. In 1942, at the age of seventy-three, he was elected councillor for Dogford ward.

Royton Industrial Co-operative Society's No. 4 branch at Birchencroft, now home to Power Tool Warehouse, was built in 1897. The Co-op built several branches throughout Royton at Middleton Road, Dryclough, Longsight, Shaw Road, Chadderton (which replaced the branch at Luzley Brook) and Summit.

Glen Grove, originally to have been called Co-operative Terrace, was comprised of twenty-four houses and was built by Royton Industrial Co-operative Society in 1899. They were built back-to-back with Birchencroft Terrace, which had been built by the society three years earlier.

A family gathering at Glen Grove, with several generations of the family present, *c.* 1905. They may have gathered to celebrate a christening, perhaps that of the little boy in the second row back, third from the right. All Saints church can be seen in the background.

Part of the family celebrations consisted of a street party. Everyone is wearing their best clothes. Note the celery in jars on the table, usually a feature of Sunday meals.

Higher Oozewood Farm. Royton Urban District Council purchased the farm from the executors of Joseph Milne's estate in 1920 in order to use some of the 106 acres to build local authority housing. The farm was rented out, the last tenant being Mr Fred Schofield. When he retired in the mid-1960s the farm was not re-let. The farmhouse was eventually demolished and the houses at the bottom of Tandlewood Park were built on the site.

Oozewood housing estate was the first to be built by the local authority. The site was acquired on 18 September 1920. Under the 1919 Housing Act, seventy-six houses were built at Oozewood, and a further fifty were built under the Housing Act of 1924.

Repairing the tram tracks on Rochdale Road, June 1936. A tragic accident occurred here in the early hours of one morning, when members of the repair gang were struck by a car. Two of the workmen died while the others were injured.

The Halfway House and dray wagon, Rochdale Road, in 1917. Aptly named the New Inn when it opened in the 1830s on the new turnpike road, it changed its name to the Halfway House soon afterwards. The public house was noted for its bowling green, now the car park.

Further up Deep Cutting, Rochdale Road, c. 1900. The grounds of Thorncliffe House are on the left.

Looking down towards Royton from Deep Cutting, Rochdale Road, *c.* 1910.

Thorncliffe (on Rochdale Road) was the home of John Rowland, a cotton manufacturer whose father owned Orleans Mill and Park Mill in Oldham. John Rowland leased the land in 1861 and Thorncliffe was built soon afterwards. In 1860 the family partnership had been dissolved and John went on to build his own mill, the Gresham, in 1862. John's son Arthur sold Thorncliffe in 1918 to Richard Greenhalgh, who died in 1936. His daughters in turn sold the house in 1938 and it was demolished soon afterwards.

Deep Cutting, Rochdale Road in 1938. On the left are the flat-top houses which were under threat of demolition in 1968 after the inside wall of one of the houses collapsed. After an agonising wait of six months, the houses were given a reprieve. They were eventually demolished around 1982.

The Pleasant Inn in 1925, when Thomas Ramsbottom was the landlord. A horse trough can be seen to the right.

Rochdale Road, looking towards Rochdale. The Pleasant Inn is on the right.

James Duckworth's grocer's shop at Summit. The shop closed in the 1970s.

Looking down Rochdale Road. The Summit public house, on the left, had a bowling green at the rear. A No. 7 tram is on its way from Hathershaw to the terminus at Summit.

Two tram cars at the Summit terminus. The left-hand tram is Rochdale tram No. 87, while that on the right is Oldham Corporation tram No. 22 on the No. 7 route to Hathershaw. No. 22, a totally enclosed double-decker, entered service in 1924/5. It was the second Oldham tram to bear this number, the first being a single-deck car which was withdrawn in the early 1920s.

A cobbled Fir Lane, with Low Crompton Road on the right. Behind the house was Dogford Mill, built by William Taylor and first mentioned as 'Cowgate Mill' in the 1805/6 Royton rate books. It was four storeys high and four windows long, and was powered by water. The Bolton 'spinning mule' was first introduced here in Royton, and steam power was added in around 1824.

Fir Lane Zion Primitive Methodist chapel is situated just over the Royton boundary in Crompton, but is considered by most local people to actually be in Royton. The chapel began in a weaver's loft, running over a number of cottages at the Top o' t' Knowl in 1833. Eventually the decision was made to construct a chapel on Fir Lane. The opening services were held on two consecutive Sundays, 28 May and 4 June 1865. In 1905 the chapel was enlarged with the addition of a Sunday school extension.

The Rising Sun off-licence, also in Compton, was situated halfway up Fir Lane on the left-hand side. The shop was run by Thomas and Mary Ellen Coleman, who had three children (Winifred, Vera and Thomas Junior). As well as selling Oldham Brewery ales, the shop also sold pottery and items of hardware.

Castleton Road in May 1961. All the cottages on the left were demolished in 1962/3 under a Council clearance order. Gravelhole Mill (to the rear of the cottages) was also demolished as part of a scheme to create a new 'garden village' of ninety-five houses and bungalows. Of the old village, only the Turks Head public house, seen in the background, and the Wesleyan chapel remain.

Looking up Castleton Road from the opposite direction in May 1961.

five

Work and Play

Thorp Mill in Thorp Clough, allegedly the first cotton mill to be built in Lancashire (in 1764). Ralph Taylor converted several cottages into a water mill, which was used for carding cotton. Later the mill was converted to steam power. The engine house, with its 16hp engine, was on the opposite side of the lane and the shaft ran over the road to the mill. The mill was later converted back into cottages

Elly Clough Mill, Holden Fold, *c.* 1880. This mill, seen astride a tributary of the River Irk, was a small water-powered mill built before 1817. By 1832, when the mill was owned by John Holden, a 10hp engine had been installed. In 1852 it was owned by Wheeler, Cope & Co. and in 1861 by John and James Clough. The mill ceased production in the 1930s and has since been demolished.

Holden Fold Mill, owned by the Holden family of Royley House, was a water-powered mill which, by 1832, was powered by a 12hp engine. A weaving shed was added in 1880. From 1959 until 1981 the Holden Fold Manufacturing Co. occupied the mill. It is now occupied by Intertrade Engineering and Ashton Windows Co.

Lion Mill on Fitton Street was built in 1890 as a sister mill to the Bee and King Mills. It ceased production in 1967 and went into voluntary liquidation the following year. The mill remained empty until 1969 when it was occupied by the Wellcome Foundation Ltd, manufacturing surgical wool and other similar products, and the Shiloh Group who used it as a distribution centre. Shiloh PLC still occupies the mill.

Holden Fold Mill, and Shiloh Mills No. 2, 1 and 1a. Shiloh No. 1 mill was built on the site of an old wooden mill of the same name that had been built in 1788. The original mill was occupied between 1838 and 1852 by John and Thomas Holden's company, and from 1861 by Rothwell, Scragg & Rothwell. In 1870 it was destroyed by fire. In 1874 the Shiloh Spinning Co. was floated by eleven local men, who then purchased the site on Holden Fold.

Shiloh No. 1 mill took two years to build. Asa Lees of Oldham supplied the machinery. The engine, from the old wooden mill, was 'traded in' as part payment for a new one. The mill began production in 1877. By the mid-1880s the 26,460 spindles were in full production. In 1888 a second mill (No. 1a) was constructed containing 9,144 spindles, followed by Shiloh No. 2 between 1899 and 1901 with 74,748 spindles. This was increased to 101,460 in 1905 by the addition of another storey.

The final mill on the site, technically in Chadderton, was the Elk Mill, christened 'Tommy's folly' by a local newspaper. The Elk Mill was built in 1926/7, designed by A. Turner. It was the last mule-spinning mill to be built in Lancashire. Shiloh Nos 1 and 1a were closed in 1953 and demolished four years later. Shiloh No. 2 closed in 1959 under the government reorganisation scheme and was demolished from 1965 onward. In 1967 the tower fell on the office block, causing extensive damage. It was finally demolished in 1976. A residential estate and retail park have now been built on the site.

Grape Mill was designed by T.W. Jenkins in 1905 for the Grape Mill Co. Ltd, who already owned the Vine Mill. The first brick was laid on 23 April 1905 and the mill was in operation a year later. In 1949 it became part of the Royton Textile Corporation Ltd, and production ceased in 1963. Sold to Higham's Ltd, it continued to spin cotton until July 2002. Higham's retain an office and warehouse on the site, while Powerplay Textiles occupies the rest of the mill.

Belgium Mill cardroom hands in March 1904.

Opposite, above: Mules, big piecer, minder and a little piecer at Roy Mill in the early 1900s. The little piecer was probably a half-timer, spending half the day working in the mill and the remainder of the day at school. Note the mill is lit by gas mantles.

Opposite, below: Fir Mill, High Barn Street, designed by A. Turner in 1906 for the Fir Spinning Co. Ltd. The mill was extended three years later and spun cotton until 1959 when it ceased production. It was taken over by James Stott of Oldham (later Stott Benham), who renamed it Vernon Works. Stotts were major suppliers of catering equipment to hotels, restaurants and industrial groups both at home and abroad. It closed in 1996 and is now used as a warehouse by Slumberland.

Scutchers in the Cotton Blowing Room, Elk Mill. Note the belts used to drive each machine. The steam turbine drove a rope race which powered the central driveshaft. From this, belts drove all the machines. The scutchers were made by Platt Brothers in 1927.

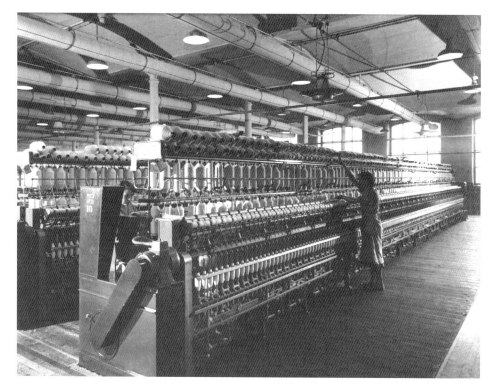

Ring spinning at Roy Mill. Ring spinning, an improved version of Arkwright's water frame, was a popular method of spinning in the USA, but it only replaced the mule as the leading spinning method in Britain in the mid-twentieth century. The ring spinning machines were manufactured by Tweedale & Smalley of Castleton, Rochdale.

A twin-tandem compound mill engine built by George Saxon Ltd of Openshaw for the Vine Mill Co. in 1898. The 22in and 44in cylinders with a 5ft stroke provided 1,800hp, which was enough to power the whole mill of nearly 100,000 spindles. The 26ft flywheel ran at 62rpm, driving thirty-five ropes.

Crates of mule cops being taken from or being delivered to Roy Mill on Rochdale Road. The horse and cart would also collect bales of cotton from the warehouse at the railway station in Royton. The mill ceased production in 1981 and was demolished in 1984.

There were two major textile companies in the 1920s and '30s: the Gartside Group and the Cheetham Group. The Cheetham Group, which consisted of Bee, Fir, King, Lion, and Thornham mills (and Ash mill, in Shaw), was under the chairmanship of J. B. Tattersall and later Will Cheetham. Both groups had their own day nurseries for the children of their female workers. That of the Cheetham Group was at Higher House, former home of the Mellor family, at the top of Rochdale Lane. The children were collected in their own special nursery van.

The Cheetham Group nursery at Higher House.

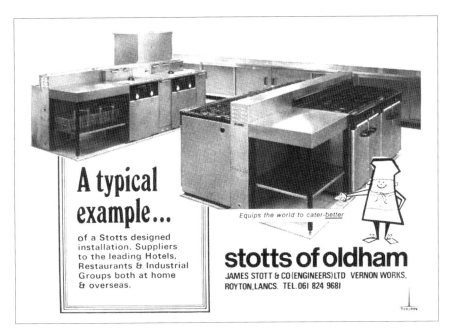

Catering equipment manufactured by Stott's of Oldham at the Vernon Works, Royton. The founder of the company was James Stott, a dental surgeon, who developed a new type of gas governor, which he proceeded to manufacture in a lean-to workshop. By 1890 it had gained over sixty awards and ultimately nearly one million various sized governors had been sold.

The first item of catering equipment, the gas kettle, was produced in 1906 and this was followed by dinner-warming ovens. Stott's moved to the former Fir Mill in 1962. In the 1960s the company was producing cafeteria counters, boiling pans, frying ranges, roasting ovens, cooking ranges and boilers. In 1979 Stott's, now part of Thorn Industries, merged with Benham & Sons Ltd to become Stott Benham. Taken over by Electrolux in 1987, the company closed in the 1990s.

Advert for James William Kent, 1902.

On the production line, assembling a 400 series cab onto a tractor unit in February 1977. In 1919 Herbert and Robert Seddon returned from the war and set up a business with Ernest Foster to operate a charabanc to take holidaymakers to the Lancashire resorts, and later as hauliers and repairers. The business developed and, as Foster & Seddon Ltd, they began to import and sell new lorries. By the late 1930s they too were building their own diesel vehicles. The Second World War interrupted production, but Seddon's did produce vehicles for civilian use along with other production for the war effort. Seddon's, for instance, produced trailers for the Ministry of Supply.

After the war Seddon Motors moved to Oldham, occupying the Woodstock Mill, a bomb-protected building previously used to produce engine parts for Spitfires. In December 1970, Seddon Motors took over Atkinson Lorries and on 1 January 1971 Seddon Atkinson Vehicles Ltd was born. In 1974 Seddon Atkinson Vehicles Ltd was sold to the International Harvester Co. of America, and in 1984 to ENASA, Spain's nationalised owner of Pegaso SA. In 1991 the Pegaso Group was bought by Fiat, and Seddon Atkinson is now part of the IVECO Group, Fiat's commercial vehicle manufacturing division. In 2002, the factory at Oldham was closed and production was transferred to IVECO's factory in Madrid.

One of the earliest lorries, a Mark 5, which was built in Royton, on a test run up Bullcote Lane. In the background is the Woodstock factory.

One of the mainstays of production at Seddon's was the dustbin wagon. Sold all over Britain, from Scotland to Cornwall, this is one of twelve refuse collection vehicles bought by the Borough of Lewisham in 1957. The Eagle 'Compressmore' body is mounted on a Mark 15 Seddon Municipal chassis and powered a Perkins P6 diesel engine with five-speed gearbox.

Crane
Fruehauf
Semi-Trailer
and Container
Market Leaders

Crane Fruehauf Trailers Ltd.,
Royton, Oldham, Lancashire.
Tel: 061-624 2441 Telex: 66648
Head Office:
Hayes Gate House, Uxbridge Road,
Hayes, Middlesex.
Tel: 01-848 0225 Telex: 262051

Crane
Fruehauf
+Boden

Left: Advert for Crane Fruehauf, *c.* 1971.

Below: The end of the production line at Crane
Fruehauf. Trailers, which had been assembled upside
down on their journey through the factory, are reversed,
to enter the paint shop on their own wheels. Crane
Fruehauf Trailers Ltd are specialists in semi-trailers and
containers. In 1970 the Royton site covered fifteen
and a half acres and employed 400 men. The company
produced an average of 150 trailers a week using a
sophisticated flow-production line, where parts came in
at one end of the factory and completed trailers left at
the other end.

Crane Fruehauf merged with Boden Trailers of
Higginshaw Road in 1968. The Crane-Fruehauf-Boden
Co. supplied half the semi-trailer market from its plants
in Royton, Norfolk and Northern Ireland. The plant in
Royton closed in 1981.

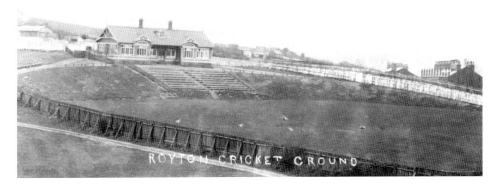

The Paddock, Royton's cricket ground, is adjacent to the original piece of land used when St Paul's Sunday school team and Shiloh Cricket Club amalgamated in 1872 to form the present club. The playing surface was dug out by out-of-work miners, and in 1878 the club acquired their pavilion from Werneth. The present pavilion was erected in 1898 and has been altered and extended in recent years. Facilities at the club improved with the construction of the bowling green in 1888 and the tennis courts in 1912.

Royton cricket team, champions of the Central Lancashire League in 1914. This was the first season the team had won the coveted honour. The league had been formed at the end of the 1891 season. In 1914, of the twenty-six games the team played, they won sixteen, lost four and six were drawn. From left to right, back row: J.G. Harrison (scorer), C. Mildenhall, J. Morton (honorary secretary and treasurer), Z. Chester, Alderman J.H. Wood (league president), T. Simpson (professional), A.S. Mellor, J.T. Littlewood, F. Morton (financial secretary). Front row: J.W. Jones, H. Seville, R. Kershaw, N. Fielding (captain), A. Groves, W. Morton, F. Walmsley.

The pavilion in around 1910. Royton sports were the summer highlight in the village. They were first held in 1871. The sports took place on the Saturday and Monday of Royton Wakes week in August, and people came from far and near to attend. So popular were they that those who could afford to go away always put off going until the Tuesday. The most popular holiday destinations from Royton station were Blackpool, Southport, Liverpool, Lytham, Fleetwood, Morecambe, the Isle of Man and North Wales.

The sports took place at the cricket ground and were organised by the cricket club. Events included foot racing, cycle racing and gymnastic displays. The large marquee on the field provided cups of tea, pork pies from Zack Brierley's, ham sandwiches etc. The sports were cancelled in 1915 for the first time in forty-five years as a result of the First World War, and have not been held since.

The Royton Hall Plate final, 3 August 1907. In 1907 6,000 spectators watched the sports events on both the Saturday afternoon and the Monday. The *Oldham Chronicle* reported some fine sprinting in the various heats of the contest for the Royton Hall Plate (also known as the Pickford Plate) for the 100yd handicap, many of the finishes being very close. The winner was L. Joss of Leeds in ten seconds; second was W.H. Howley of Broughton, and third was C. Whittaker of Paddock AC.

The high-jump event at the thirty-eighth annual Royton sports festival on 1 August 1908. There were nineteen events that year, the principal one being the two-miles walking NCAA championship, with thirteen entries. The high-jump event was won by H.S. Mellander of Sefton Harriers, who jumped 5ft 7in, while the holder A.H. Healey jumped 5ft 6in.

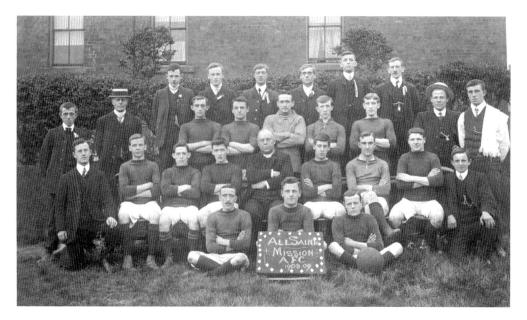

All Saints Mission AFC, 1908/9.

Royton Harriers, c. 1920. The Harriers were formed in 1898 by a group of men who got together to enter any cross–country event being held. In 1920 they won the championship of the South East Lancashire Cross-Country League, a feat they repeated in 1926. They had their own meeting place, using a small hut in Shaw Road. In 1954 the Harriers headquarters moved to Hillside Avenue and used the Westwood track for training. When the track closed, the club moved to Radclyffe School.

Royton and Crompton Golf Club in 1960. The decision to form a golf club, later to be known as Crompton and Royton Golf Club, was made in December 1907 and a site was obtained at Higher Park in Shaw. In 1913 the club decided to lease High Barn Farm, in addition to further land at High Barn in Royton, in order to build an eighteen-hole course (Higher Park had only nine holes) and the new golf links opened later that year. The purpose-built clubhouse, which was designed by Winder-Taylor, opened in 1924, replacing the one located in the old farmhouse. Further land was purchased in 1965 and the course was extended in 1967.

Royton Prize Band outside Royton Hall in 1932. That year they won first prize at Leyland parish church May festival. There were fourteen bands competing in the contest, including Boarshurst and Haydock Colliery. They won £25 and a silver medal for the conductor, Robert Cooper.

Royton morris dancing team posing with Boy Scouts on 18 July 1925, at Daisy Hill, just above Hough Bottom Cottage. The dancers had taken part in St Paul's Sunday school pageant and the crowning of the Rose Queen.

A final word of advice and good wishes after the flag had been broken by Queen's scout Barry Turner at the start of the three-day Scout Jamborette at Tandle Hill on 14 June 1958. The campers 'dug in' on Friday and Saturday to prepare for their march past on the Saturday afternoon. The salute was taken by H.W. Blomerley, Honorary Assistant County Commissioner (Scouts).

In 1952 this Mk XVIe Spitfire TE184 was presented to Royton Air Training Corps (ATC) for instructional purposes, and it stood as a gate guard until February 1967 when it was moved to RAF Bicester for use in the film *Battle of Britain*. The aircraft then had a succession of owners, and, following a rebuild, it flew for the first time since 1951 on 23 November 1990. In September 1967 a Meteor NF14 night fighter replaced the Spitfire.

The ATC was well-known for its motorcycle display team. This five-man pyramid in 1960 was made up of Vic Scriven (top), Barry Thompson (left), Steve Kenworthy (driver), Mike Hughes (right) and Tony Buck (bottom).

Edge Lane Mission's banner, followed by that of St Cuthbert's on Oldham Road, in around 1907. The Primitive Methodist chapel can be seen to the left of St Cuthbert's banner.

St Paul's church Whit procession on Oldham Road, *c*. 1910

six

Modern
Royton

One of many mill chimneys to be pulled down, Holly Mill chimney was demolished on 28 April 1962. Only two mill chimneys now remain in Royton: the Lion and the Sandy.

After the Second World War, Royton Council embarked on a massive redevelopment scheme to create a 'dream town'. Areas of the town, consisting of old terraced houses and shops, were cleared to make way for council, private and housing association development. In other areas houses were modernised and houses for the elderly and the disabled were constructed.

Holly Mill estate in October 1973. Building the estate of 224 houses, flats and maisonettes commenced in 1964 and was not completed until 1967, bad weather and a shortage of materials delaying the project by six months.

Royton Hall Park development, under construction in April 1972. The disused railway station, cotton warehouse and goods yard were bought by Royton Council in 1969, forming the final piece in the town centre redevelopment jigsaw. The £750,000 'Royton Hall Park' scheme on the fifteen-acre site would provide housing for 945 people and included this three-storey hostel for elderly people.

In addition to new council house developments, a large amount of private housing was also constructed in the 1960s and '70s. Chetwyn Avenue, part of the Thorpe estate development, was constructed in January 1976.

Royton town hall and shopping centre seen from St Paul's church spire in April 1972. The construction of the new 'Sunset Strip' shopping precinct is almost complete. The proposal to redevelop the centre of Royton was put forward in the early 1950s, approved by the Council in 1963 and the Minister of Housing and Local Government in 1966. As part of the redevelopment plans, the whole of the centre of Royton, between Rochdale Road, Market Street, High Street and Sandy Lane was to be bulldozed to make way for new shops, a supermarket and for old people's accommodation. The area to the north of Market Street was demolished first. The new precinct opened on 30 September 1971.

Market Day on 4 November 1971.

Royton and Crompton School in 2004. Royton and Crompton School was formed by the amalgamation of Royton Central School (now Highbarn) and Crompton Central School (the former Newbarn Junior School). It operated on these two separate sites until 9 September 1968, when the school moved to its present site on Blackshaw Lane. At this time it also absorbed St Anne's Church of England Secondary School. The school became a comprehensive school for eleven to sixteen year olds in 1975, and for eleven to eighteen year olds in 1980. The school lost its sixth form in 1993 with the opening of Oldham sixth form college.

Salmon Fields industrial estate in 1988. Oldham Council revealed plans for a huge one million square foot industrial estate and new road in July 1983, to be funded by Oldham Council, Greater Manchester Council and the EEC Regional Development Fund. Despite a 6,000-name petition strongly objecting to building on a greenfield site, approval was obtained from Whitehall in 1985.

Other local titles published by Tempus

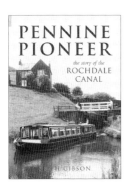

Pennine Pioneer – The Story of the Rochdale Canal
KEITH GIBSON

Rochdale Canal, the most successful of the three trans-Pennine canals, was built 200 yea
ago. Trade boomed on the canal until the beginning of the twentieth century, when the
arrival of motor transport had a dramatic effect on its importance as a trade route. It wa
formally abandoned in 1952. This book, which includes over 100 archive photographs,
follows the life of the Rochdale Canal from its inception to its abandonment, and tells c
the more recent battle for its restoration.

0-7524-3266-4

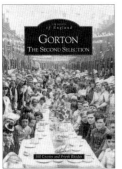

Gorton: The Second Selection
JILL CRONIN AND FRANK RHODES

This collection of over 220 archive photographs takes a look at some of the changes in
leisure, housing, business and industry which have taken place over the last century in
Gorton. It is a nostalgic look back at the pubs, cinemas, churches and schools that have
changed over the years, including poignant photographs of VE Day street party celebrati
Each picture is supported by a wealth of historical detail sure to appeal to all who know
have known, Gorton.

0-7524-2669-9

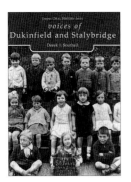

Voices of Dukinfield and Stalybridge
DEREK J. SOUTHALL

Oral history is unique in its facility to make the past accessible, and to catch the flavour
of a time and the lives of the people concerned. This carefully compiled book combines
vivid memories with the personal photographs of the interviewees, creating a valuable
and enthralling record of the first half of the twentieth century in and around this part
of Greater Manchester. The reminiscences range from childhood games to first-time job
memories of war and anecdotes of local characters, such as the man with two birthdays,
the last tripe dresser in Stalybridge.

0-7524-2679-6

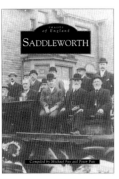

Saddleworth
MICHAEL FOX AND PETER FOX

This fascinating collection of almost 200 old photographs taken in the villages of
Saddleworth provides a dramatic insight into the life of days gone by in these hardy
communities, perched on the high borderland between Lancashire and Yorkshire. The bo
explores the history of Saddleworth, from its people and their homes to farms and mills,
includes archive images of dramatic events, such as the fire that destroyed Greenfield Mil
1914. This book will appeal to all who know this beautiful yet rugged land and would e
a journey back into its recent past.

0-7524-2275-8

If you are interested in purchasing other books published by Tempus, or in case you have difficulty finding any
Tempus books in your local bookshop, you can also place orders directly through our website

www.tempus-publishing.com